MEMORIES OF COVENTRY

ALTON DOUGLAS

DENNIS MOORE

ADDITIONAL RESEARCH BY

JO DOUGLAS

© 1987 Alton Douglas, Dennis Moore, Jo Douglas
© 1994 Alton and Jo Douglas.   5th Impression
ISBN 1-85858-032-3
Published by Brewin Books, Doric House,
Church Street, Studley, Warwickshire B80 7LG
Printed at Alden Press Limited, Oxford and Northampton, Great Britain

ALTON DOUGLAS is probably best known as the author of several best-selling books and for the three years he was quizmaster (and co-writer) of the top-rated BBC Midlands TV series "Know Your Place". However, he is also a TV and radio character actor, ex-professional comedian, showbiz/jazz book and record reviewer, TV and radio commercial voice-over artist, one-time 5th Royal Inniskilling Dragoon Guards trombonist, the voice behind several cartoons and children's toys, etc.

He has appeared in virtually every major theatre in the U.K. (including the London Palladium) and was responsible for hundreds of television studio warm-ups.

His television appearances include "Know Your Place" (3 series), "Angels", "Seconds Out", "A Soft Touch", "Muck and Brass", "The Golden Shot", "The Knockers", "The Original Alton Douglas", "Nights at the Swan", "Watch This Space", "The Barmaid's Arms", "Open University", "Property Rites", "Big Deal", "Newshound", "Murder of a Moderate Man" and "The Bretts". His radio plays include "Mr Peabody and the Beast", "Troupers", "The Family That Plays Together, Stays Together", "You Can't Judge a Book by Looking at the Cover", "Sorry Goodbye and Get Stuffed" and the award-winning "Guernica". He was also the archives and stills consultant for the centenary video "Made in Birmingham".

Since 1981 Alton has had 22 books published:

"Memories of Coventry"
"Coventry at War"
"Coventry: A Century of News"
"Memories of Stratford-upon-Avon"
"Birmingham at Work"
"Birmingham Shops"
"Birmingham Remembered"
"Memories of Birmingham"
"Birmingham at War Vol 1"
"Birmingham at War Vol 2"
"Dogs in Birmingham"
"Joe Russell's Smethwick"
"The Black Country at War"
"Memories of the Black Country"
"Memories of Dudley"
"Memories of Shrewsbury"
"Memories of Walsall"
"Memories of West Bromwich"
"Memories of Wolverhampton"
"Memories of the Wrekin and Beyond"
"Alton Douglas's Celebrity Recipes"
"Alton Douglas's Know Your Place"

****** **LOOK OUT FOR NEW TITLES EACH YEAR** ******

CONTENTS

INTRODUCTION

BY 1950 (in no small measure due to the effects of the recently ended war) Coventry had changed and grown so swiftly that the modern city was in danger of forgetting the glories and beauty of the old city. As time has moved to the present, it has become even more apparent that memories of the old Coventry are more precious than ever and need to be preserved. This book aims to do just that.

Towards the end of the 1st century AD, there was no settlement of tribes or families in Coventry. The land, being clay, was difficult to work and much of the ancient forest had to be cleared first. In contrast, the sandy soil and tree-free areas of Baginton and Corley were much more hospitable, and it was these that were eventually to grow into the habitation we now know as Coventry.

There are numerous spellings of early and late Coventry including: Cofentreium, Coventreo, Coventria, Coventre, Cofantreo, Coventrev, Couentre, Coventrey, Covingtre and Covintry. The last part of the word certainly suggests a tree and the first part seems to refer to a person named Cofa. Who he or she was and why they planted a tree or inspired the planting of a tree within the ancient settlement remains a mystery. In 1043 Leofric, Earl of Mercia, with his wife, Godiva, founded a monastery in Coventry for an abbot and 24 monks. The king, Edward the Confessor, was greatly in favour and rewarded them both by granting a charter confirming the gift. The real beginnings of Coventry stem from the foundation of this monastery for, as it grew in influence, greater resources were required, so attracting pilgrims, craftsmen and merchants into the community.

No mention of Godiva could fail to include the legend of her famous ride, undertaken to free the local inhabitants from certain taxes levied by her husband Leofric. There is no "Peeping Tom" in the original legend but present-day citizens perpetuate his existence.

Its central situation favoured the growth of Coventry, and the River Sherbourne (at one time much bigger than it is now) provided water supplies and a source of power for the mills. Local stone from Whitley and Cheylesmore assisted building and good, arable land was close at hand for farming and stock-rearing. At the time of the Domesday Book (1086 AD) Coventry was still a very small village containing a mere handful of people but by 1500 AD prosperity was at its height. Cloth, wool, leather and metal goods, soap and needles were the early trades.

When Henry VI visited the town in 1451 he complimented the mayor and burgesses on the excellence of their local governing, urging them to continue this good work and to maintain the peace. The king's parting gift was to confer on Coventry the singular honour of being a county.

By the early 18th century the town was large and well populated, doing great trade in cloth, ribbons, clocks and watches and silk-weaving, the latter remaining a major industry until the invention and manufacturer of bicycles, motor-cycles, motor-cars and areoplanes.

Population growth is significant: under 13,000 in 1749, just over 16,000 in 1801, near 37,000 in 1851 and in 1901 almost 70,000. By 1932, 167,046 inhabited the city, 258,211 by 1951, whilst present numbers exceed 316,000. Boundaries became contentious issues in 1838, resulting in an Act of Parliament (1842) which took away Coventry's status as a county and re-defined the boundaries as a city enclosing 1,486 acres.

On the night of November 14, 1940, a clear, cold, beautiful night, came the greatest air-raid so far directed by the Germans against an English provincial city in the war which had begun in 1939 and was to last until 1945. St Michael's Church, the old Cathedral, was destroyed with only its great tower and spire remaining intact, but by 1962 a new Cathedral, built right against the old, was consecrated. In 1987, for the first time in 100 years, the bells of the old Cathedral rang out officially to mark the 25th anniversary of the event.

Reconstruction of the bomb-scarred city gave opportunities for planners to open up the city to traffic (by use of an inner ring-road) yet at the same time reducing cross-city motor traffic. Further steps were taken to provide pedestrian-only precincts where shoppers were free from motor traffic.

With this post-war planning and the eventual realities came hope for the citizens and workers of Coventry — a hope born out of new industries where the old had become outmoded and a belief that the city would once again hold its head high with pride in the achievements of its craftsmen, its managers and its professions.

BEGINNINGS

UNTIL the early part of the 18th century, education was neither universal nor compulsory and what educational facilities existed were not funded by or controlled by the State. Only the wealthy could afford to pay fees. However, the monks at Leofric's priory, as part of their alms-giving, started a school for poor children. After 1303 the priory also maintained a public grammar school. A typical school day in the summer ran from 6 am to 11 am followed by an afternoon session from 1 pm to 5 pm — quite a rigorous routine. Holidays were brief and occasional half-days were granted for special reasons only. There were no organised games and the main subjects were music and the classics. Charity schools came into prominence between the end of the 17th century and the middle of the 19th century. Among these were three for girls — The Blue Coat School, Southern and Craner's and the Freemen's Orphan School. Foundations for boys were Baker, Billing and Crow's, Katherine Bayley's in Little Park Street and Fairfax's in Spon Street. A School of Design was opened in 1843 with particular reference to the ribbon industry. Twenty years later a School of Art was built in Ford Street.

Fairfax's (Green Gift) School, c. 1887

School band of Katherine Bayley's School (Blue Gift), Little Park Street, c. 1887

Bablake School, c. 1887

Blue Coat School, c. 1900

Warwickshire Education Committee.

Balsall Street Central School.
Nr Coventry. ~~Department.~~
10·ix· 1926

Chas George Viner has attended this School since 18·ii·1924. He has been regular & punctual in attendance, well-behaved and attentive to his work; he has made steady progress.

His brother, Raymond Viner has been in regular attendance since 9·xi·1925·

W.F.E.Seeley.
Headmaster.

Chas Viner just promoted to Std IV
Raymond .... Sen.Infants.

Miss Steane's School, Moor Street, Earlsdon, 1931

Barker Butts School, 1931

Stoke Park Secondary School, May, 1936

4

7

COVENTRY TECHNICAL COLLEGE

Junior Technical School

FORM REPORT

Name.......Jenks....... Form...4A... Position...10... No. in Form...18...

Times present...136... Times absent...0... Next term commences......April 17th 1941

Subjects	PERCENTAGES		Position	Remarks	Master's Initials
	Term	Exam.			
English	69		5	Good.	D.BH.
History & Geography	63		8	F. good. A quiet worker.	CCh.
Mathematics	74		11	F.G.	H.J.Y.
Metalwork	56		13	Good. a little more speed.	
Woodwork	61		15²	Good.	WSG.
Engineering Drawing	56		10	Good	L.H
Mechanics	60		15⁼		R.M.H.
Physics	80		4	Working very well	S.H.
Chemistry	66		11	Quite good.	K.H.D
German	88		2	V.good	

PHYSICAL EDUCATION	SCHOOL ACTIVITIES	CONDUCT
Posture ...	...	Detentions... 1
Swimming ... He is now trying much harder	...	Report Cards... 0
Gymnastics ... is far keener	...	Corporal Punishment... 0
Games ... than before ...	...	

Remarks... A good term's work.

....Headmaster.

J Wilson ....Principal.

Signature of Parent... D. Jenks.

S3841/1000/2/40 (y)

Radford (temporary) Branch Library, October, 1931

Story hour at Stoke Branch Junior Library, 1948

Priory High School receiving instruction at Stoke, 1948

This library & its books are under the protection of the Boys & Girls of Coventry

King Henry VIII School Sports Day, 1954

Stoke Secondary Modern Boys' School Choir, 1955

Manor Park School, Cheylesmore, 1958

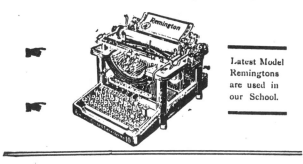

9th N. Coventry (Keresley) Company of Girl Guides' 21st celebrations, 1955

The Coventry Battalion of the Boys' Brigade, 1964

Alderman Harry Weston says "Au Revoir" to a group of Cheylesmore Scouts as they leave for camp in France in 1953

(Receipt, top left)

'Phone: PRIDDY 284

PRIDDY STORES
(Proprietors: H. & I. Glover)

Grocery, Provisions, etc.

PRIDDY, Nr. WELLS

11th Coventry Scouts   Aug 11 1960

1	12 Bread	@ 1/-		12	0
2	2c Pork Saus	@ 2/10	2	16	8
3	12 Tomatoes	@ 1/6		18	0
4	1¾ Tea	@ 7/-		12	3
5	2 Peaches	@ 11/6	1	3	0
6	1 Sugar	@		11	6
7	5 tins Cocoa	@ 4/5	1	2	1
8	14 Cornflakes	@ 1/6½	1	1	7
9	18 Sardines	@ 1/4½	1	4	9
10	16 tins Jordy Cream	@ 3/2	2	10	8
11	12 tins Prince Rice	@ 1/-		12	0
12	56 tins Ham Sausage	@	2	17	9
13	36 tins SR Meat	@ 2/4	4	4	0
14	10 tins Oats	@ 2/2	1	1	8
15	8 tins Jutland	@ 1/3		10	0
16	7 lb Plum Jam			9	5
17	7 " Straw			11	8
18	7 " AP			11	2
19	7 " Marmalade			9	7
20	2 cut. Potatoes		2	7	6
21	14 lbs Onions	@ 3½		9	11
22	14 " Carrots	@ 8		9	4
23	28 " Marrows	@ 1/3	1	15	0
24					
25	0++ – 19		£29	1	6

13

The staff of Wheatley Street Infants' School, 1895

THEY ALSO SERVE

COVENTRY never lagged behind other cities and towns in social work and it was in 1878, for example, that the founder of the Salvation Army, General William Booth, sent from London two women to begin the Army's work in the city.

The Marchioness of Reading formed in 1937 the WVS (later the WRVS) to perform a number of welfare duties that might arise from any national emergency. This service, in company with organisations such as the St John Ambulance and British Red Cross Society, to name just a couple, continue their excellent work.

The Coventry & Warwickshire Hospital came into existence in 1837, but it is surprising, considering the amount of infectious desease at that time, that the city's first isolation hospital was not opened until 1871.

A new library building was mooted in 1868 but this met with some resistance — "the money could be much better spent on a good soup kitchen." Only through the benefaction of Andrew Carnegie, the Scottish-American steel magnate, were the branch libraries at Earlsdon, Foleshill and Stoke built in 1913. Mr Carnegie was granted the honorary freedom of the city in 1914 for his generosity.

Meeting of Public Assistance Committee, c. 1930

City Council, 1928

City of Coventry Fire Brigade, 1911

16

The Standard Fire Brigade, c. 1910

17

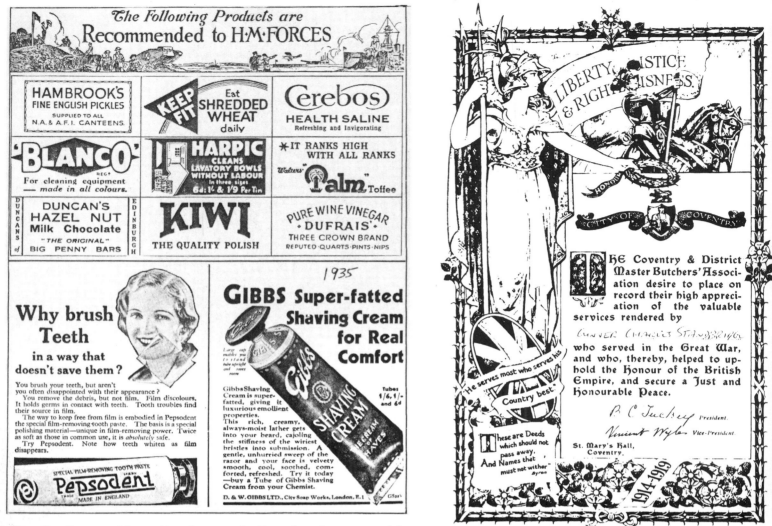
South Lancashire Regimental Band play outside Coventry Station, April 23, 1915

Coventry City Salvation Army Band, May 8, 1920

Barrack Square Police inspection, September 21, 1915

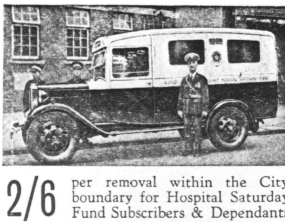

Wounded soldiers in Coventry and Warwickshire Hospital, 1916

Student nurses at Coventry and Warwickshire Hospital, Christmas, 1939

British Red Cross A team, c. 1960

St John Ambulance preparing for possibility of war, Alexandra Theatre, Lower Ford Street, January, 1939

St John Ambulance Gaumont Cadets' 1st anniversary of Division, 1953

St John Ambulance, Alfred Herbert Division, c. 1950

Tea party for WVS members with the much-loved Pearl Hyde third from right, c. 1942

. . . and they also serve! Coventry & District Licensed Victuallers' Association visit Arthur Guinness Son & Co (Park Royal) Ltd, London, November 24, 1959

IN TOWN

DURING the Middle Ages, those ten or eleven centuries intervening between ancient and modern times, Coventry had dwelling-houses varying according to the social status of their inhabitants. The lord of the manor occupied his manor house just within the city walls at Cheylesmore; the rich merchants dwelt in their stone houses; timber buildings, well constructed, housed the middle-class craftsmen and shopkeepers; very basic, slumlike houses were the lot of the labourers.

Through good and bad times, neglect has taken its toll of the smaller dwellings. When aerial bombardment added destruction to decay it was inevitable that controlled demolition would also become necessary to accommodate the urgent need for re-planning.

Larger buildings, such as churches, have survived the bombs and the planners' designs. Ford's Hospital and Bond's Hospital, both with 16th century origins, are protected, being graded I and II respectively, and every effort will continue to be made to preserve them. A number of buildings in Spon Street are, in their turn, considered to be of special architectural or historic interest and are therefore protected.

Hearsall Lane/Broomfield Place, 1935

Barracks Square, January 26, 1950

Chapel of St James and St Christopher, Spon Street, 1898

Court 38 (North Side) Spon Street, c. 1957

A court in Bond Street due for demolition, October 26, 1956

Fleet Street, c. 1905

Fleet Street, 1952

Burges, 1930

Nos. 1-3 Burges, 1921

oss Cheaping, looking towards Bishop Street, 1892

onmonger Row, looking west from Bull Ring towards Cross Cheaping, 1935

FLASHBACK ON FIFTY YEARS OF FURNISHING SERVICE

1900 Woodhouse's 1950
Golden Jubilee

You are cordially invited to join in celebrating our Golden Jubilee and share in the full benefits of six glorious Golden Opportunities

OPPORTUNITY No. 2. THE NEWEST MODEL KITCHEN EQUIPMENT

Gas Woodhouse & Son

post this coupon

20/21, Cross Cheaping
COVENTRY

Also at Birmingham and Walsall.

NOW for Illustrated Furniture and Radio Catalogue FREE from your nearest branch

NAME _____
ADDRESS _____

Cross Cheaping, looking towards Burges, c. 1936

Hales Street, 1935

Hales Street, 1952

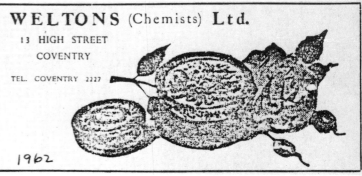

Weston Street/Swanswell Street, c. 1966

Co-op Building, Smithford Street, 1933

Smithford Street, c. 1905

Temporary shops, Smithford Street, c. 1946

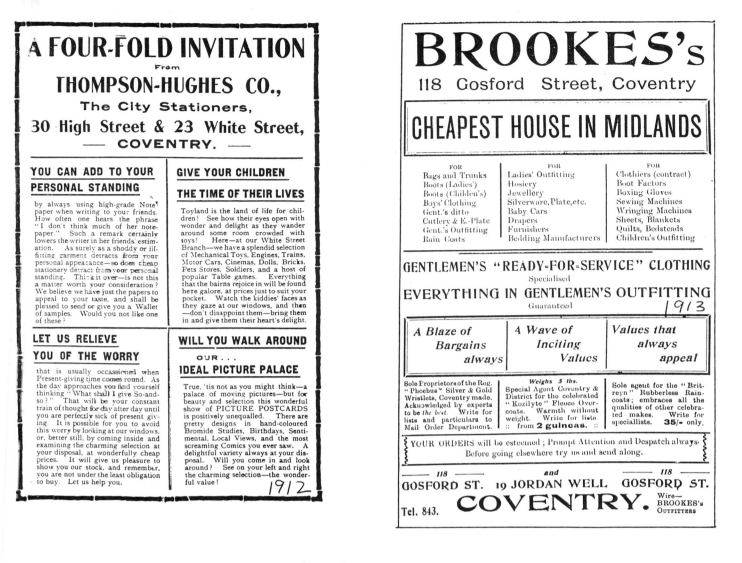

Broadgate, 1935

33

Broadgate, c. 1898

34

The new Cathedral under construction, March 6, 1961

High Street, 1910

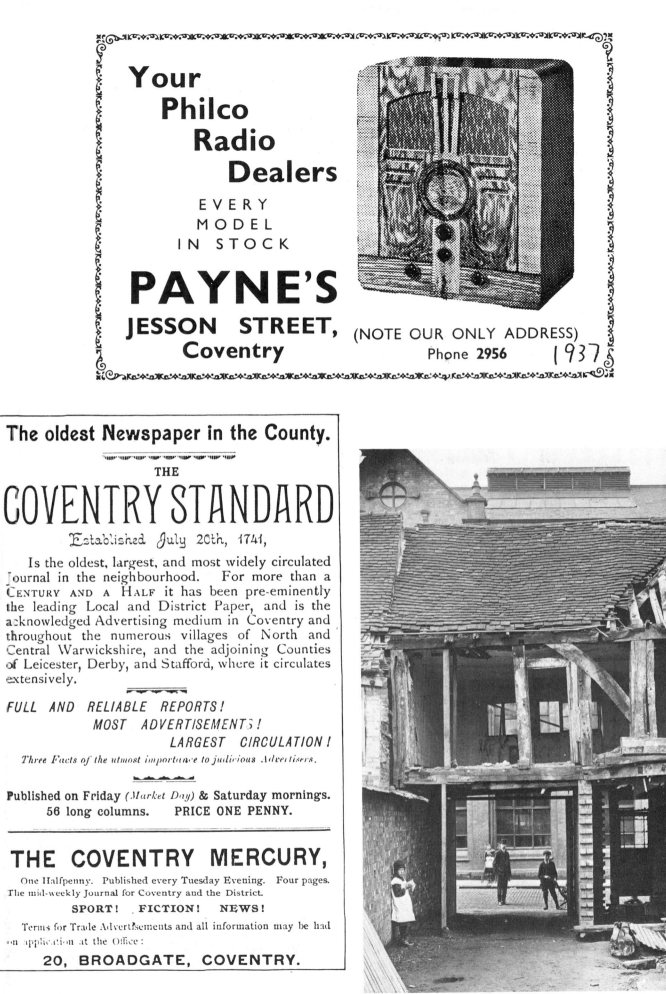

Yorkist Meeting House, Little Park Street, 1920

Cow Lane / Little Park Street prior to demolition in 1937

Bull Ring and Butcher Row, seen from Ironmonger Row, 1935

Butcher Row, c. 1912

Butcher Row, 1935, prior to demolition to provide for a new Trinity Street

Butcher Row, 1934

Little Butcher Row, 1935

Hertford Street, 1929

Hertford Street, 1910

44

Hertford Street, c. 1910

West Orchard, 1912

Temporary shops, Earl Street, 1955

Coliseum Buildings, Jordan Well, c. 1928

Coventry Station from Eaton Road, 1902

Gosford Street, 1916

Ansty Road, c. 1932

Binley Road, looking towards Far Gosford Street, c. 1910

Far Gosford Street, from Paynes Lane, January 4, 1960

ON THE MOVE

JAMES STARLEY (born in 1830) came to Coventry in 1861 and began to manufacture sewing-machines, but seven years later he was persuaded to make French bicycles with wooden wheels and iron tyres that soon earned the tag "bone-shaker." He improved these with steel wheels and solid rubber tyres, a large front wheel and a small rear one. So was born the "penny-farthing." Only the fittest of men could ride these, so Starley invented his tricycle. The "safety bicycle" soon followed for use by females as well as males and Coventry's flourishing cycle trade grew. The motor cycle and motor car industry in Coventry inherited a skilled workforce from the bicycle factories and further fame followed.

Not everyone could afford his own machine so the Coventry Tramways Co began in 1882 a steam tramway from the centre to Bedworth. Hills proved a problem until 1895 when steam was superseded by electricity. Later, Bell Green, Stoke, Chapelfields and Earlsdon were given routes. Motor buses started in 1912 and worked with trams until war damage to tracks in 1940 saw the tram system being abandoned.

Dual carriageways, flyovers, bypasses and motorways assured the motor car speedy journeys and Coventry a thriving trade.

The railway came to Coventry in 1838, connecting with London and Birmingham and later, in 1850, the line to Nuneaton was completed.

In July, 1935, when flying was attracting much interest, the city established an aerodrome at Baginton, on land that had been municipally owned since 1897. This wisdom and foresight is evident today in a fine, well-run airport.

James Starley, c. 1875, founder of the cycle trade in Coventry

"SALVO" SAFETY

NEW ILLUSTRATED CATALOGUES POST FREE.

STARLEY BROS.,

ST. JOHN'S WORKS, COVENTRY.

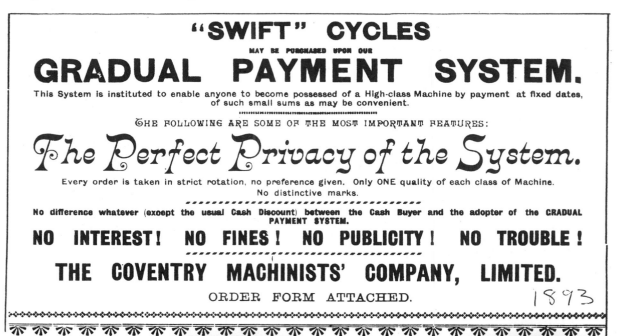

Coventry-made Starley bicycles on show at Crystal Palace, 1900

GOYS FIRST
OLD STYLE 1817

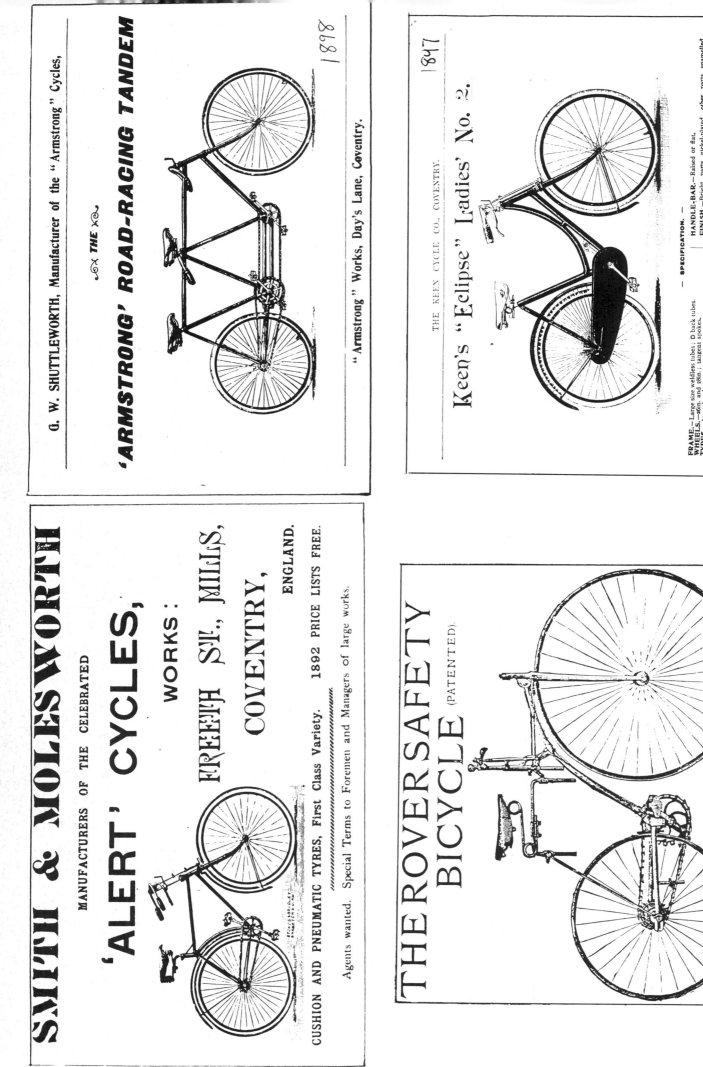

G. W. SHUTTLEWORTH, Manufacturer of the "Armstrong" Cycles,

THE

'ARMSTRONG' ROAD-RACING TANDEM

1898

"Armstrong" Works, Day's Lane, Coventry.

1897

THE KEEN CYCLE CO., COVENTRY.

Keen's "Eclipse" Ladies' No. 2.

SPECIFICATION.

FRAME.—Large size weldless tubes; D back tubes.
WHEELS.—26in. and 28in.; tangent spokes.
TYRES.—As ordered.
DRESSGUARD.—Of silk cord; leather gear case.
BRAKE.—Rubber shoe.

HANDLE-BAR.—Raised or flat.
FINISH.—Bright parts nickel-plated, other parts enamelled black; if any other colour, and lined, 10s. extra.
WEIGHT.—31 lbs.

PRICE.—With Dunlop, Palmer, or Fleuss tyres £22 10 0
  " Beeston or Warwick tyres 20 10 0

OLDEST FIRM IN THE TRADE.

SMITH & MOLESWORTH.

MANUFACTURERS OF THE CELEBRATED

'ALERT' CYCLES,

WORKS:

FREETH ST., MILLS, COVENTRY,

ENGLAND.

CUSHION AND PNEUMATIC TYRES, First Class Variety.   1892 PRICE LISTS FREE.

Agents wanted.   Special Terms to Foremen and Managers of large works.

THE ROVER SAFETY BICYCLE (PATENTED).

52

Early examples of the motor-makers' art, The Motor Manufacturing Co Ltd, c. 1898

THE NEW PENNINGTON AUTOCAR.

I am now prepared to accept orders in large quantities for my New Patent Autocar,
AS ILLUSTRATED ABOVE.

THIS IS THE ONLY MACHINE:

Made to carry four people, fitted with a seven horse-power motor.

That will *not* blow up, or where passengers do not run risk of being set on fire.

(All machines using a carburetter, or lamp, are liable to blow up, or be set on fire, at any moment, sacrificing life and property.)

That can carry its full load up a steep hill at a high speed.

That can be stopped on a steep hill, and start again uphill with a full load.

That can run up a long hill without emitting forth smoke or steam.

That can run for several hours without using lubricating oil on running parts.

That can run over tram lines at any angle with perfect safety.

That is fitted with unpuncturable tyres.

Is the lightest machine built to carry four people.
Is the strongest machine built to carry four people.
Is the best running machine for all-round work.
Is ready to start at a moment's notice.
Has less loss of power between motor and driving wheel than any other machine built.
Has less odour than any other machine built.
Has less vibration than any other machine built.
Has less noise than any other machine built.
Why buy an Autocar that you may have to set aside in a few days, owing to the contravention of the new Board of Trade Regulations.
Orders also accepted for three-wheeled machines to seat two people.
And for four-wheeled Victorias, to seat either two or four people, with overhead hood.

For Prices and Full Particulars regarding their sale in Great Britain, address —

E. J. PENNINGTON, Motor Mills, COVENTRY.

Coventry Motor Club, Charterhouse, c. 1902

**A Riley Fore-car of 1903, inspected by the Library Committee,
1955**

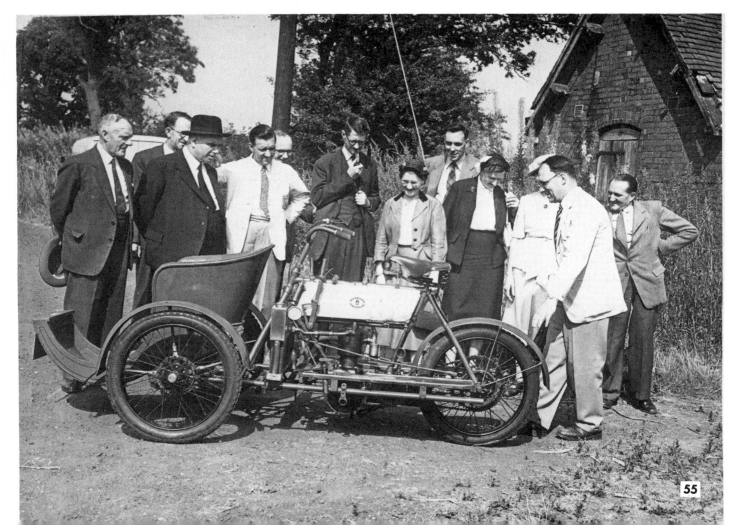

Coventry Station yard, showing Daimler cars and a Daimler bus, 1921

Calcott Bros Ltd, 1921

Horse bus, c. 1900

Maudslay bus in Walsgrave Road, 1914

Humber Hotel, c. 1914

Open-top motor bus in use on Stoke Heath/Hearsall Common route, c. 1919

Corporation Transport, c. 1927

Dennis bus, used for country services, Pool Meadow, 1936

Coventry Transport

Serving a population of 215,000, operate

TRAMCAR SERVICES:

No. 1	Bedworth	....	Cov. Station	every 10 minutes
„ 2	Longford	....	Broadgate	„ 5' „
„ 5	Bell Green	....	Cov. Station	„ 10 „
„ 6	Broad Street	....	Broadgate	„ 5 „
„ 8	Uxbridge Avenue		Broadgate	„ 8 „

BUS SERVICES:

No. 1	Stoke Heath	....	Maudslay Road	every 10 min.
„ 2	Green Lane	....	Radford	„ 10 „
„ 3	Stoke Aldermoor		Hen Lane	„ 6 „
„ 4	Stoke Heath	....	Coundon	„ 10 „
„ 5	Binley	....	Coundon	„ 10 „
„ 6	Lenton's Lane or Alderman's Green		Earlsdon	Hourly
„ 6	Walsgrave	....	Earlsdon	every 10 min.
„ 7	Allesley	....	Pool Meadow	„ 12 „
„ 8	Tile Hill	....	Pool Meadow	„ 15 „
„ 9	Broad Lane	....	Broadgate	„ 20 „
„ 10	Brownshill Green		Pool Meadow	„ 30 „
„ 11	Glendower Avenue		Pool Meadow	„ 10 „
„ 13	Willenhall	....	Pool Meadow	„ 20 „
„ 14	Inner Circle	....		„ 30 „
„ 16	Keresley	....	Pool Meadow	„ 40 „
„ 17	Baginton	....	Pool Meadow	„ 40 „
„ 18	Burton Green	....	Pool Meadow	Approx. hourly
„ 19	Berkswell	....	Pool Meadow	Approx. every 2 hours

Subject to adjustment in accordance with traffic requirements.

AT YOUR SERVICE

1937

Vernon Street/Paynes Lane, c. 1935

Broadgate, c. 1938

Tram conductresses, Broadgate, 1915

Coventry Station, c. 1879

Coventry Station, October 23, 1959

October, 1945

AT WORK

THE author of "Robinson Crusoe," Daniel Defoe, visited Coventry in the early part of the 18th century and he was most complimentary about the diligence and expertise of local craftsmen. "The city is large and populous, having a great trade consisting chiefly of the weaving of tammy (worsted cloth) and ribbons. It is the very image of the City of London," and he went on to describe the beauty of the timber buildings and quaint streets.

The making of cloth was foremost in trade, employing weavers, drapers, tailors, dyers, fullers and shearmen. Until modern industry brought fame and fortune to the city with the manufacture of cycles, motor cycles, cars, aeroplanes and electrical equipment, early metal trades provided an admirable training ground for future artisans. Among these older trades were needle-making, brass, pewter and gold fashioning, watches and clocks. Millers, brewers and victuallers were always in demand as were the products of the glass and tile makers, the hatters and the glovers.

Telephone 766.   THE   *1912*

Northampton Brewery Co.
Ltd.,

ARE NOTED FOR THEIR

SPECIAL BRIGHT ALES
IN CASK AND BOTTLE.
Caterers especially are requested to try these Beers.

Wines and Spirits of the finest quality.

Offices and Stores for Coventry and Leamington Districts:

5 St. Nicholas Street, Coventry.
E. C. GOULSTON, Local Manager.

Great Horseless Carriage Company works, c. 1897

Swallow workers, 1930

Swallow factory, 1930

Armstrong Siddeley demonstration car (for self-change gearbox), Holyhead Road, c. 1932

63

Maudslay Motor Co Ltd, Park Side, c. 1910

Testing re-conditioned engines at Triumph, July 3, 1959

Massey-Ferguson, c. 1956

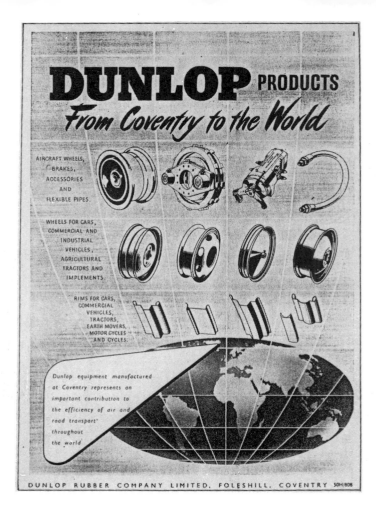

Daimler, c. 1914

Alvis, 1930

Alvis, 1920

Calcott Bros Ltd, April, 1921

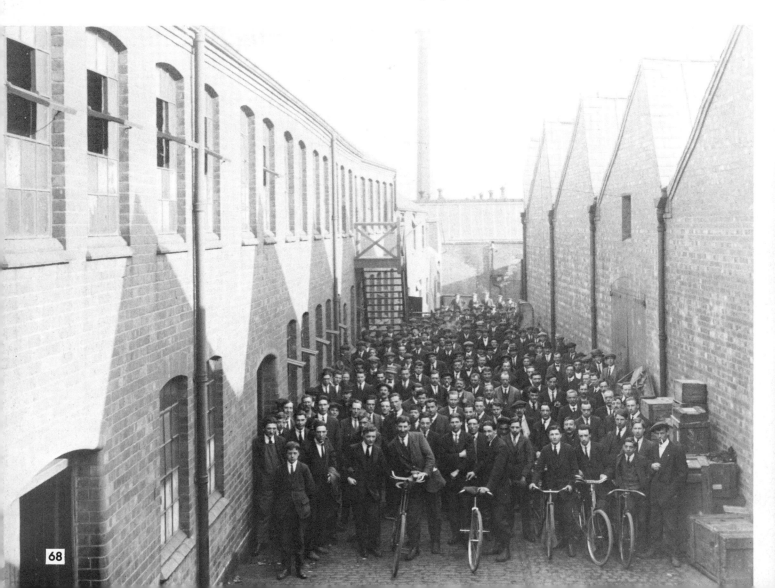

The Foundry, Coventry Evening Telegraph, 1959

Coventry Evening Telegraph, 1960

White & Poppe Ltd, c. 1908

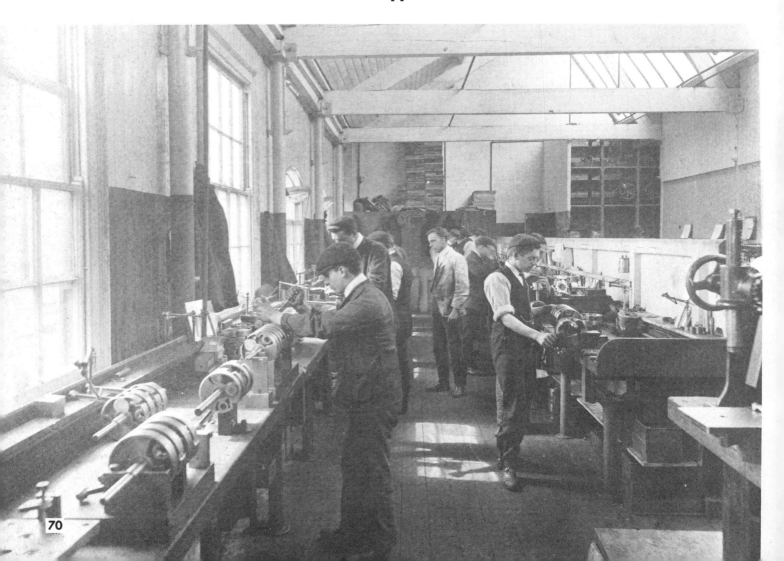

The complete service

for Private business, Public Telephone Administrations, Electric Power Companies, Railways and other public undertakings at Home and throughout the World.

1950

TELEPHONES

EXCHANGES (Telephone & Teleprinter)

RADIO COMMUNICATION

GECOPHONE JUNIOR
Intercommunication System

REMOTE SUPERVISORY CONTROL

TRANSMISSION SYSTEMS
Line or Radio, Telephone or Telegraph

For everything in Telecommunications and Remote Supervisory Control

consult

G.E.C.

The largest British Electrical Manufacturing Organisation in the World

THE GENERAL ELECTRIC COMPANY LIMITED
TELEPHONE, TELEVISION AND RADIO WORKS — COVENTRY
Telephone: COVENTRY 4111 (10 lines) · Telegrams & Cablegrams: "SPRINGJACK, COVENTRY"

GEC 1908

MAGNETO CALL TABLE TELEPHONE.

K 8085

Comprising a Hand Microtelephone, with "Hunningscone-Deckert" Transmitter and Double-pole "Ring" Receiver, Nickel-plated Ornamental Cradle Switch, Induction Coil, Generator with two extra large Permanent Magnets, Polarized Call Bell, Four-conductor Flexible Connecting Cord, and Wall Rosette with Terminals and plate-type Lightning Arrester with perforated Mica Insulation. All external metal parts Nickel-plated and Lacquered. The Magnets are provided with four Rubber Feet, to prevent damage to desk or table.

Price **£5 0 0**

Peel-Conner Telephone Works (later GEC), c. 1922

Workers leaving GEC Telephone Works, 1939

Errington Watch Works, Holyhead Road, c. 1920

"Brink," the last horse of the Coventry Co-operative Society, with head stableman and driver, April 23, 1956

Market Square, c. 1910

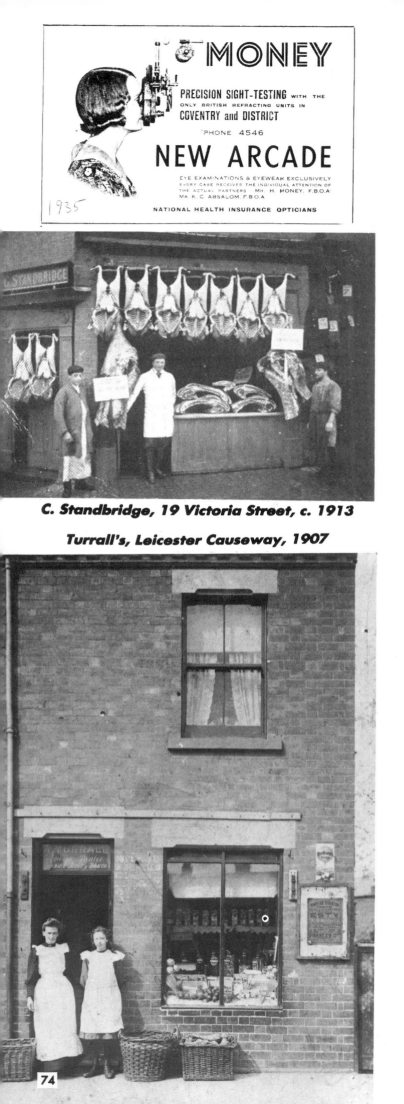

C. Standbridge, 19 Victoria Street, c. 1913

Turrall's, Leicester Causeway, 1907

54 Spon Street, 1941

AT PLAY

FOR centuries poaching for salmon or game was rife though forbidden by national and local laws, yet in Coventry bull-baiting and bear-baiting were openly encouraged by the city authorities. Cock-fighting was not favoured by them yet it survived even into living memory. Archery was not allowed in the streets towards the end of the 15th century, so special mounds or butts were constructed for safe practice. Barkers' Butts Lane and The Butts mark the sites of two of these. By the early 16th century mere craftsmen were forbidden to play bowls, quoits or football because they would then tend to neglect their work upon which their livelihood depended. Horse-racing became popular in the 18th century, meetings being held in the park adjoining the city. Coventry Football Club (Rugby Union) was founded in 1873 and did not lose a game until the last match in the 1876/77 season. Early games were played at the Old Bull Fields until the move to The Butts in 1880. After World War I came the move to Coundon Road. The Golf Club came into being in 1887, with courses at Pinley Fields and Whitley Common. The move to Finham Park took place in 1908.

Coventry & North Warwickshire Cricket Club was set up in 1851. Prominent past members included Lord Kenilworth and R. E. S. (Bob) Wyatt, the former Warwickshire and England cricket captain.

Coventry City Football Club Ltd (the Sky Blues) was formed by employees of Singer and played under that Company's name until 1898. Coventry City had slipped to the newly-created Fourth Division by 1952, yet, under Mr Derrick Robins (chairman) and Mr Jimmy Hill (manager), the team eventually swept thrillingly into the First Division. The Club's record attendance of 51,455 was achieved at the home game against Wolves on Saturday, April 29, 1967. In 1987 the Sky Blues won both the FA Youth Cup and the FA Cup.

Cinemas in Coventry, as elsewhere, were most popular and the super-cinemas, for example The Gaumont Palace (opened in October, 1931) and The Rex (opened in 1937), were greatly patronised. Prior to the Second World War local firms who had flourishing social clubs for their young, skilled workers provided value-for-money entertainment. The less fortunate paid 1/6d or half-a-crown (7½p or 12½p) for a dance at the Rialto or attended a 2d (1p) open-air dance, known as a "hop," at the Red House in Red Lane.

Coventry City FC, Division III Champions, 1963/64

Cheering crowds acclaim Coventry City FC, Division II Champions, 1966/67

Coventry Football Club (Rugby Union), 1945/46

Iliffe Athletic Club Rugby XV, 1904/5

Courtaulds Hockey Team, c. 1920

Warwick Road Cricket Club, champions of the Coventry & District Free Church Cricket League, 1904/5

Godiva Harriers, 1913

Coventry cyclists, 1892

Alfred Herbert Cycling Club, 1932

The Bees, 1966

Members of the Coventry Motor Club at Kenilworth, 1925

Opening of Priory Street Baths, 1894

Gosford Swimming Pool, August 8, 1955

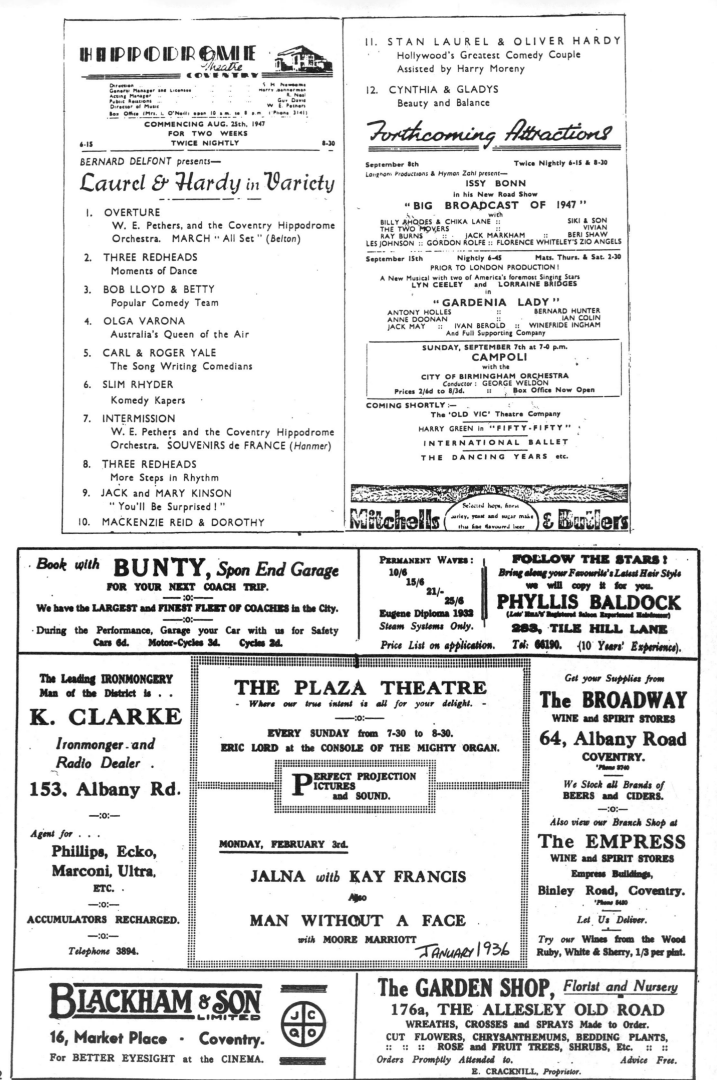

The Coventry Repertory audience on the hottest night of the year, Hales Street, July 12, 1934. The play was "Ten Minute Alibi"

The Barron Knights at the Locarno, 1965

Hippodrome Orchestra, 1945

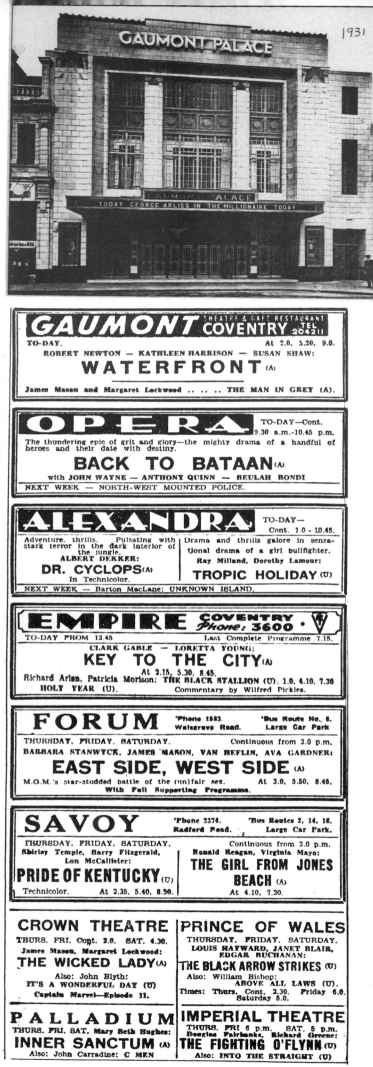

1931

GAUMONT PALACE

TODAY GEORGE ARLISS IN THE MILLIONAIRE TODAY

GAUMONT COVENTRY
THEATRE & CAFE RESTAURANT TEL 204211

TO-DAY.   At 2.0, 5.20, 9.0.
ROBERT NEWTON — KATHLEEN HARRISON — SUSAN SHAW:
WATERFRONT (A)
James Mason and Margaret Lockwood .. .. .. THE MAN IN GREY (A).

OPERA
TO-DAY—Cont.
9.30 a.m.-10.45 p.m.
The thundering epic of grit and glory—the mighty drama of a handful of heroes and their date with destiny.
BACK TO BATAAN (A)
with JOHN WAYNE — ANTHONY QUINN — BEULAH BONDI
NEXT WEEK — NORTH-WEST MOUNTED POLICE.

ALEXANDRA
TO-DAY—
Cont. 1.0 - 10.45.

Adventure, thrills. Pulsating with stark terror in the dark interior of the jungle. **ALBERT DEKKER:**	Drama and thrills galore in sensational drama of a girl bullfighter. **Ray Milland, Dorothy Lamour:**
DR. CYCLOPS (A) In Technicolor.	**TROPIC HOLIDAY** (U)

NEXT WEEK — Barton MacLane: UNKNOWN ISLAND.

EMPIRE COVENTRY
Phone: 3600
TO-DAY FROM 12.45.   Last Complete Programme 7.15.
CLARK GABLE — LORETTA YOUNG:
KEY TO THE CITY (A)
At 2.15, 5.30, 8.45.
Richard Arlen, Patricia Morison: THE BLACK STALLION (U). 1.0, 4.10, 7.30
HOLY YEAR (U).   Commentary by Wilfred Pickles.

FORUM
'Phone 1583.   'Bus Route No. 8.
Walsgrave Road.   Large Car Park.
THURSDAY, FRIDAY, SATURDAY.   Continuous from 2.0 p.m.
BARBARA STANWYCK, JAMES MASON, VAN HEFLIN, AVA GARDNER:
EAST SIDE, WEST SIDE (A)
M.G.M.'s star-studded battle of the (un)fair sex.   At 3.0, 5.50, 8.45.
With Full Supporting Programme.

SAVOY
'Phone 3374.   'Bus Routes 2, 14, 16.
Radford Road.   Large Car Park.

THURSDAY, FRIDAY, SATURDAY.	Continuous from 2.0 p.m.
Shirley Temple, Barry Fitzgerald, Lon McCallister:	Ronald Reagan, Virginia Mayo: **THE GIRL FROM JONES BEACH** (A)
PRIDE OF KENTUCKY (U) Technicolor. At 2.35, 5.40, 8.50.	At 4.10, 7.20.

CROWN THEATRE	PRINCE OF WALES
THURS. FRI. Cont. 2.0. SAT. 4.30. James Mason, Margaret Lockwood: **THE WICKED LADY** (A) Also: John Blyth: **IT'S A WONDERFUL DAY** (U) Captain Marvel—Episode 11.	THURSDAY, FRIDAY, SATURDAY. LOUIS HAYWARD, JANET BLAIR, EDGAR BUCHANAN. **THE BLACK ARROW STRIKES** (U) Also: William Bishop: **ABOVE ALL LAWS** (U). Times: Thurs. Cont. 2.30. Friday 6.0. Saturday 5.0.
PALLADIUM THURS. FRI. SAT. Mary Beth Hughes: **INNER SANCTUM** (A) Also: John Carradine: C MEN	**IMPERIAL THEATRE** THURS. FRI 6 p.m. SAT. 5 p.m. Douglas Fairbanks, Richard Greene: **THE FIGHTING O'FLYNN** (U) Also: INTO THE STRAIGHT (U)

86

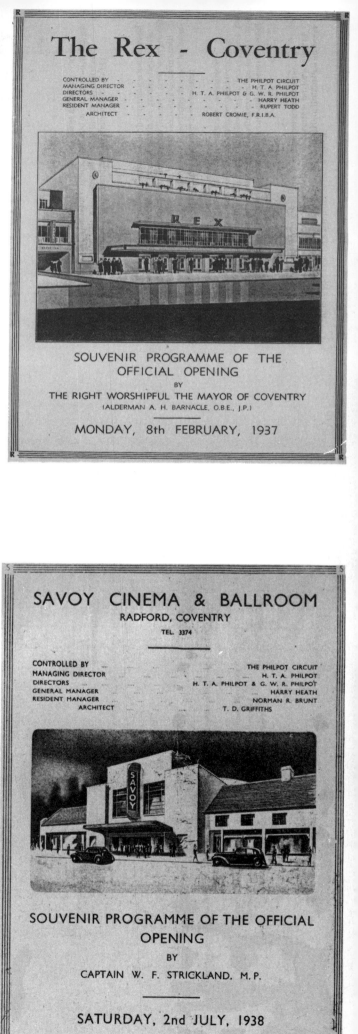

The Rex - Coventry

CONTROLLED BY   THE PHILPOT CIRCUIT
MANAGING DIRECTOR   H. T. A. PHILPOT
DIRECTORS   H. T. A. PHILPOT & G. W. R. PHILPOT
GENERAL MANAGER   HARRY HEATH
RESIDENT MANAGER   RUPERT TODD
ARCHITECT   ROBERT CROMIE, F.R.I.B.A.

REX

SOUVENIR PROGRAMME OF THE OFFICIAL OPENING
BY
THE RIGHT WORSHIPFUL THE MAYOR OF COVENTRY
(ALDERMAN A. H. BARNACLE, O.B.E., J.P.)

MONDAY, 8th FEBRUARY, 1937

SAVOY CINEMA & BALLROOM
RADFORD, COVENTRY
TEL. 3374

CONTROLLED BY   THE PHILPOT CIRCUIT
MANAGING DIRECTOR   H. T. A. PHILPOT
DIRECTORS   H. T. A. PHILPOT & G. W. R. PHILPOT
GENERAL MANAGER   HARRY HEATH
RESIDENT MANAGER   NORMAN R. BRUNT
ARCHITECT   T. D. GRIFFITHS

SAVOY

SOUVENIR PROGRAMME OF THE OFFICIAL OPENING
BY
CAPTAIN W. F. STRICKLAND. M.P.

SATURDAY, 2nd JULY, 1938

EVENTS

A CHARTER of incorporation was granted to Coventry by Edward III in 1345, being the first of its kind in the country, giving powers to the corporation to elect a mayor, bailiffs and other leading citizens to preside over the city. In 1451 Henry VI raised Coventry to a County of the City, this status being removed in 1842 whilst still retaining the title "City." It became a County Borough in 1888 and, in 1953, coronation year, Queen Elizabeth II conferred the dignity of a Lord Mayoralty on the city. She laid the foundation stone of the new cathedral on March 22, 1956. Earlier, on Christmas Day, 1946, a radio exchange programme was put out by the BBC linking Coventry with the continental cities of Arnhem, Caen, Stalingrad and Warsaw, which led to exchange visits between Coventry's Mayor and those of Arnhem and Caen. This friendly gesture prompted similar exchanges between other towns and cities in Western Europe.

Spon Street, New Year's Eve, 1900

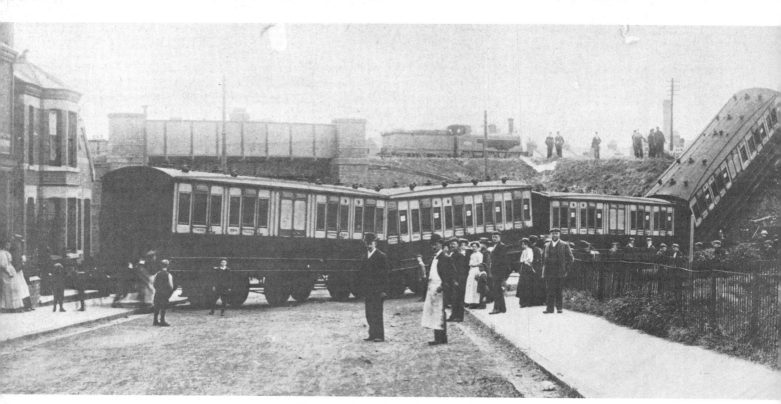

Albany Road, Earlsdon, July 4, 1904

Coventry Station, November 21, 1959

Tenants ejected from condemned property in Well Street, 1912

*Closure of Little Butcher Row by the Mayor, Alderman Payne,
January 1, 1936*

Visit of Queen Mary and Princess Royal to inspect the munition works. At Canon Baillie's home, Vicar's Croft, Davenport Road, September 18, 1917

The Duke of York (later King George VI) comes to open the new Council House in Earl Street, June 11, 1920

Princess Elizabeth (now the Queen) opens the rebuilt Broadgate, May 24, 1945

Part of the crowd awaiting the arrival of King George VI and Queen Elizabeth, Broadgate, April 5, 1951

CITY OF COVENTRY

CIVIC DINNER

Thursday, 29th August, 1946

AT

THE BRITISH RESTAURANT
ALBANY ROAD, COVENTRY

To mark the occasion of
the Visit of

The Commanding Officer, Officers & Men of

H.M.S. "Argonaut"

Coventry's Adopted Ship

7 p.m.

Counc. J. C. LEE-GORDON, J.P.
Mayor

SOUVENIR

OF THE

—OPENING—

OF THE NEW

HUMBER WORKS

AT

COVENTRY

March 12th, 1908.

The occasion is the laying of the foundation stone for the Empire Theatre, June 30, 1906. The famous actress Ellen Terry sits in the back of the car

Installation of Mrs Pearl Hyde as the first lady Lord Mayor of Coventry. This was the first televised mayor-making ceremony anywhere, May 23, 1957

Lord Iliffe lays the foundation stone of the new Coventry Evening Telegraph building in Corporation Street, November 21, 1957

Opening of Corporation Street, June 13, 1931

Coach-and-four outside the Old Posting-House, High Street, c. 1900

Godiva procession in Broadgate, 1907

Outing of cycle and motor workers, 1900

Wayzgoose (an outing) for Coventry printers, c. 1910

Tank Bank Week, Broadgate, 1918

Coventry Carnival, 1928

Godiva Pageant and Carnival, 1929

White & Poppe outing to Holt Fleet, June 1909

CITY OF COVENTRY EDUCATION COMMITTEE

CAMERA PRINCIPIS

OPENING OF THE NEW TECHNICAL COLLEGE BY HIS ROYAL HIGHNESS THE DUKE OF YORK, K.G. DECEMBER 10th, 1935

Armstrong Siddeley Band and contingent near No. 2 Gate prior to the unveiling of the War Memorial in the Memorial Park, 8 October 1927

Charter celebrations, 1945

Staff and guests at the prizegiving at The Birches (residence for nurses of the Keresley branch of Coventry & Warwickshire Hospital), 1952

British Thomson Houston workers visit Newdigate Colliery, 1960

GREEN AND PLEASANT

THE fact that population numbers within the city appear to be falling slightly points to the availability, within quite short distances, of green fields, farmlands and rural villages which tempt city dwellers to set up home outside the tight inner-city boundaries. The hatred of ribbon development along roads going out from the cities in the 1930s caused Coventry and Birmingham to confer together with the county of Warwick with a view to preserving an undeveloped area, a green belt, around the two cities. Thankfully this policy is being maintained, for under the Town & Country Planning Act (1932) the city gained powers to this end.

Rear of Ford's Hospital, October 6 1931

The city seen from Greyfriars Green, c. 1885

The Fair on Pool Meadow, c. 1920

The Forge, Coat of Arms Bridge Road, Stivichall, c. 1860

Coat of Arms Bridge, Stivichall, 1943

The Grove, Kenilworth Road, c. 1910

Canley Milk Bar, August 12, 1969

Bedworth Road, Longford, c. 1935

Swanswell, 1906

wanswell, Coventry

13453

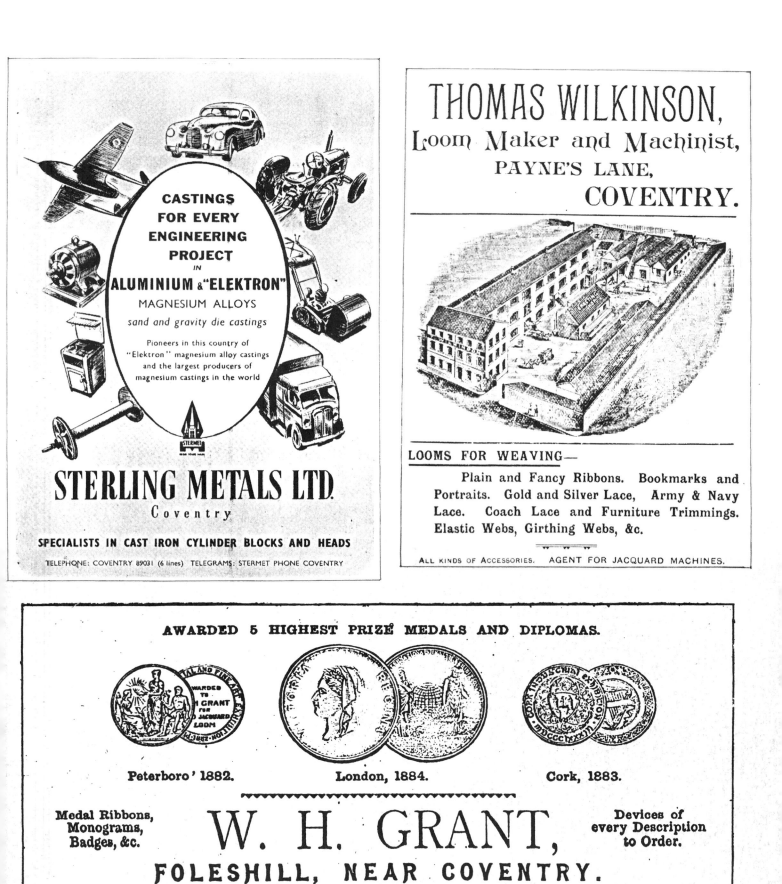

ACKNOWLEDGEMENTS

(for providing photographs, for encouragement and numerous other favours)

Neil Allen; Alvis Ltd; Jo Ault; Austin Rover; Mary and Jim Boulton; Dave Carpenter; Coventry Division of the West Midlands Police; Coventry Evening Telegraph Staff; Coventry Fire Station; Coventry Local Studies Library; Beryl and Ted Cross; Jim Garside; GEC Telecommunications Ltd; Clive Hardy; John Harrison; Jaguar Cars Ltd; Pat and John Jenks; Anne Jennings; Margaret and Jack Lathbury; Massey-Ferguson; Philip Murphy; Museum of British Road Transport, Coventry; Ken Narborough; Ray Norton; Pat Pearson; Victor Price; Gil Robottom; Rolls-Royce Heritage Trust; the Salvation Army; John Spencer; Stoke Park School and Community College; Gordon Stretch; Edna and Raymond Viner; Ron Williams.

Please forgive any possible omissions. Every effort has been made to include all organisations and individuals involved in the book.